7 Questions

YOU SHOULD ASK YOURSELF
Every Day

MASTER KEYS TO UNLOCKING
THE GREATNESS WITHIN YOU

Mike Smalley

7 Questions You Should Ask Yourself Everyday
Master Keys To Unlocking The Greatness Within You

Copyright © 2009 by Mike Smalley

Unless otherwise indicated, all Scripture references are from the New King James Version of the Bible (NKJV).

ISBN: 978-1-61584-292-6

Hall of Honor

The following made the printing of this book possible. I encourage all who are benefited by this book to call their names in prayer!

Bryan and Casie Fratt
Georgia Thomas
Donna Burton
Darren and Kimberly Bishop
David and Dorothy Spradlin
Anthony and Eileen Pena
Sammy and Mary Pena
Sandra Dinkins
Robyn Collins
Gwendolyn and JW Fields
Paul and Maudie Lawyer
Arlena Sickles
Linda F. Baker
Daniel Pickering
Mauricio and Angela Lastra

Diego and Isabella Giovanna
Mignona Cote
David and Elaine Gentry
Bonnie York
Mary Jo Brinkley
Fred and Brenda Taylor
Ken Anthony
Howard Lull
Donna Brown
Terry and Glenda Butler
Joe and Kim Fears
Craig Clay
Pastors Glynn and Carolyn Davis

"Many, While Focusing On Their Future, Have Failed To Evaluate Their Present."

Dr. Mike Smalley©

Table of Contents

"Every Conversation Releases Your Giftings. . . Or Feeds Your Weakness."

Dr. Mike Smalley©

Introduction:
The Most Overlooked Path
To Success Is A Question

Questions Are The Golden Key To Life!

Never mismanage your energy pursuing answers.

The "room of answers" is always blocked by a door. *Questions* are the key that grants access.

Jesus understood this master principle as early as the age of 12: "*And it came to pass, that after three days they found him in the temple, sitting in the midst of the doctors, both hearing them and asking them questions.*" (Lk 2:42, 46)

Later, as an adult Jesus would publically establish this law of Kingdom Order. . . *the key to all receiving is a question!*

". . . Ask, and you will receive . . ." (John 16:24b)

Never complain about what you are not receiving if you have not been willing to ask. Asking must always come *before* receiving. . . before receiving an answer, a miracle, or a breakthrough.

The difference between people is not the answers they know, but the questions they become willing to ask.

Never wait "hoping to receive." Start the acceleration of your breakthrough by asking!

10 Benefits Of Questions

1. **Questions Document Your Humility**.
   Asking is an admittance someone knows something you don't.

2. **Questions Document Your Reaching.**
   Millions confuse desire with pursuit.

3. **Questions Reveal What You Believe Is Important**. . . like the man who cried out to Paul "What must I do to be saved?"
   (Acts 16:30)

4. **Questions Are A Link To Master Mentors Looking To Plant the Seed of Experience Into Worthy Soil.**

5. **Questions Are What God Uses To Qualify Receivers.** "And whatever things you ask in prayer, believing, you will receive." (Mt 21:22) ". . . you do not have because you do not ask." (James 4:2b)

6. **Questions Birth Favor**. "The speech pleased the Lord, that Solomon had asked this thing.
(I Kings 3:10)

7. **Questions Are Often The Only Difference Between Those Who Are Told Yes And Those Who Are Told No.** ". . . I don't fear God or care about people, but this woman is driving me crazy. I'm going to see that she gets justice, because she is wearing me out with her constant requests!'"
(Lk 18:4b-5 NLT)

8. **Questions Decide Who Gains And Keeps Access**. "Now when the queen of Sheba heard of the fame of Solomon. . . she came to test him with hard questions. . . Solomon answered all her questions. . ."
(I Kings 10:1, 3)

9. **Questions Reveal The Deception Of Your Enemy.** "And they said to Him, "By what authority are You doing these things? But Jesus answered and said to them, "I also will ask you one question. . .The baptism of John —was it from heaven or from men? Answer Me."
(Mark 11:28-30)

10. **Questions Decide Promotion.** "And so it was, when they had crossed over, that Elijah said to Elisha, "Ask! What may I do for you, before I am taken away from you?" Elisha

said, "Please let a double portion of your spirit be upon me." (2 Kings 2:9)

Your success is being decided by the kinds of questions you are continually asking.

Questions. . . you ask your boss.

Questions. . . you ask a mentor.

Questions. . . you ask God.

Questions. . . you ask yourself.

The answers you desperately need are always on the other side of the right question.

Questions unlock passion and fresh awareness of the greatness within you. *Ask often.*

I wrote this book because I care deeply about your dreams and goals. I know the Holy Spirit will use these 7 questions to move you into your next season and unlock the greatness within you.

A wounded world is waiting for your anointed entry into its darkness. You. . . *are needed.*

Start asking questions. . . and start living with answers!

Question 1:
Do The People I Love The Most Know It?

There Is No Substitute For The Power Of Expressed Love!

"Love never fails. . ." (I Cor. 13:8a)

Love is a responsibility, as much as it is a pleasure. Love is like a garden. . . God makes us responsible to keep it free from weeds.

Our life and actions continually send a message to those around us.

Is the message you are sending clear?

As easily as love can grow, it can also be misunderstood.

Every parent knows the frustration of working six days a week "for their children," only to be jaded by the comments, "You're never home. . . you don't care what happens to us."

Love can be miscommunicated as easily as it can be ignored, overlooked or under expressed. Thus, the reason to master communication between ourselves and those we deeply love. Never assume you will have "another chance" to document your love.

Love can only be expressed within the gift of time.

My Boxing Coach

As a young man years ago, I joined our city's boxing team. My coach was a retired professional heavyweight fighter from the 1940's. He had made headlines around the world and now, in his golden years of retirement, was teaching young men the master secrets of his career.

A bond quickly grew between us. I knew his affection for me as a protégé ran very deep, as did my respect and admiration for him.

One day, I arrived at the gym for my workout to discover he was not there. It is the first time I remember hearing the word "cancer." A short time later, my beloved coach was dead.

His funeral was the first I would ever attend. The day of his burial was especially sad for me because of a hidden secret. Weeks earlier, I had been invited to attend a school function at a local skating rink. My parents were still at work, so to attend the event, I had to walk with a friend 5 miles to the rink.

My friend took me through a shortcut with an unexpected surprise. I was on the street my boxing coach lived on! I recognized it from the times my father had driven the aged coach home. I stood in front of his house, gripped in fear, but wanting to go inside to say hello and express my love and appreciation for his life. I knew he was dying.

Sadly, because of the shyness of a young boy and the fear that his wife, whom I had never met, would not receive me, I convinced myself to leave without knocking and told myself there would be another time to see him.

I was wrong.

He died before I could.

Love is meant to be expressed. *Now.*

King Solomon said it best, "An open rebuke is better than hidden love." (Prov 27:5 NLT)

The Harvest of Friendship

Recently, my brother and I, along with two childhood friends drove 10 hours round trip in a single day to visit a boyhood friend battling a serious illness.

All of us have ministries or businesses and lead very active lives, but *nothing was more important on that day than letting Keith know we cared.*

The regrets of my past have been a continual motivator to end each day answering this most important question. . . "Do the people I love the most know it?"

It's too easy to express love. It's too costly not to.

I urge you today to remember the words of James 4:14, *"Life is like a vapor."* You cannot control the actions and reactions of another, but you can decide the words you say and the love you express. . . a*nd how often you express it.*

God wanted to remove any doubt in our mind of His love toward us. The sacrificial death of His Son on the cross is a continual reminder of His extravagant love!

Express love clearly. Show love often. Prove love daily. Take risks. *Remove any doubt.*

"Do the people I love the most know it?" It is one of the 7 questions you should ask yourself everyday.

Question 2:
Is The Holy Spirit Pleased With Me?

No One's Approval Matters More Than The Holy Spirit!

The Holy Spirit is the most vital relationship in our life. His approval should matter more to us than the approval of any other relationship.

He never hides His feelings, or camouflages His emotions. His opinions do not change. *He craves dialogue.* Nobody talks more than He does.

He reminds us of the words of Jesus.
"But the Helper, the Holy Spirit, whom the Father will send in My name, He will teach you all things, and bring to your remembrance all things that I said to you." (John 14:26)

He is the believer's constant companion. *"And I will pray the Father, and He shall give you another Comforter, that He may abide with you forever."* (John 14:16 KJV)

The Holy Spirit knows when His presence is celebrated and when it is not. He is the voice of the Godhead on the earth today.

Sadly, many attend churches where months and even years go by without a message being preached about His necessary role in their life.

Yet, it is impossible to live a victorious Christian life without Him.

God will not allow any human relationship in your life to bring you total peace and contentment.

If He did, the role of the Holy Spirit would become unnecessary.

Talk to Him continually.

Ask Him to draw you into His Word.

Continually share with Him your burdens, your struggles and your fears.

His mentorship is irreplaceable.

Your joy and fulfillment in life will always be proportionate to your obedience to the Holy Spirit. When He is pleased with your life, He continually surrounds you with His favor.

Never confuse an encounter with God in the past with the Holy Spirit's approval of your present.

5 Ways To Know The Holy Spirit Is Presently Pleased With Your Life

1. **Inner Peace.** Peace is an indication of His pleasure. *"For the kingdom of God is not eating and drinking, but righteousness and peace and joy in the Holy Spirit."* (Rom 14:17)

2. **Outward Joy.** Joy is the gift he deposits as a reward for spending time in His presence. *". . .In Your presence is fullness of joy. . . "* (Ps 16:11b)

3. **Great Favor** Acts 2:46-47 documents the day the Holy Spirit fell, favor emerged. *". . . having favor with all the people. . ."*

4. **The Entry Of New Relationships That Extend Your Influence On The Earth.** Divine Promotion stops when the Holy Spirit has shifted His approval.

5. **The Flow Of Creative Ideas He Sends Into Your Spirit.** The Holy Spirit speaks often when He knows He will be obeyed.

The Holy Spirit longs to be your constant companion. . .your *very best friend.* He will never pressure you to perform at a level you are incapable of. He will never permit you to remain confused as to his instructions and desires for your life.

His plans for you are incredible! His thoughts toward you are constant. His opposition to your enemies remains consistent.

Thousands across the earth speak to him at the same time and in different languages. . .yet He remains unconfused and delights in answering each simultaneously.

Allow Him to guide your every step. Consult Him first on every major decision. He is the most vital relationship in your life.

"Is the Holy Spirit pleased with my life?" It is one of the seven questions you must ask yourself every day.

Question 3:
Am I In The Center Of My Life Assignment?

God Does Have A Plan For Your Life!

"For I know the plans I have for you," declares the LORD, "plans to prosper you and not to harm you, plans to give you hope and a future." (Jer 29:11 NIV)

Many refer to it as "your purpose," or God's perfect will. My mentor, Dr. Mike Murdock, calls it *The Assignment.*

Your assignment is the problem God created you to solve on the earth. . . what God placed you here to do. Your assignment is unique. It is what you are commissioned to accomplish . . . what you are supposed to become. . . what you are supposed to fulfill.

Do you know what it is?

If not, are you seeking to know?

Are you studying to discover?

Are you *asking* the right questions?

A Sad Reality

Recently, I was given some statistics showing 80% of American workers either do not enjoy or even hate their present job.

We are living in a generation that has stopped reaching for their dreams. *Even many Christians are content to drown in the river of mediocrity while claiming to follow the One who walked on water!*

God has designed us so when we are fulfilling His assignment for us on the earth, every pleasurable thing around us is magnified!

Your sense of self-worth, inner fulfillment and personal accomplishment are directly linked to your life assignment.

Nobody has your life assignment!

The gifts and talents the Holy Spirit placed inside you are special for the life he designed with you in mind. God needs your gifts and talents. God designed your unique personality. *You matter!*

What is your life assignment?

Can you write it out in a single sentence?

It Happened In East Texas

God "called" me into the ministry when I was 14. As excited as I was to know a small portion of what the Lord wanted for my life, it was *many years* before I knew specifically how and what the details of this calling would be. I remained unsure of many things for years. . . but I kept pursuing until the full revelation came.

If you don't yet know what your life assignment is. . . *don't feel condemned.*

Ask. . . the Holy Spirit for clarification.

Sit. . . at the feet of seasoned mentors.

Evaluate. . . what you love, what you hate, and what problem you would pay any price to solve.

Your assignment will always be linked to something you love to do, and a people you love helping.

The greatest tragedy on earth, outside of not knowing Jesus, is to live a lifetime and never discover your life assignment.

The Holy Spirit is very serious about revealing to you your assignment. Every positive emotion you are wanting in life is waiting on you at the center of your life assignment.

Expect Conflict

Satan fears your assignment. This explains much of the warfare in your life and why he so desperately attempts to surround you with wrong people, influences and doubt.

Every relationship that doesn't increase ultimately takes away.

Every task that doesn't add. . . subtracts.

Every conversation releases your giftings. . . or feeds your weakness.

God has designed you to make a major difference on the earth. Your past does not disqualify you from present influence.

Thousands are in desperate need of the gold inside of you. Discovering and fulfilling your life assignment is your greatest responsibility on the earth. Joy will always be at the center of this incredible journey.

"Am I in the center of my life assignment?" It is one of the seven questions you must ask yourself every day.

Question 4:
Who Will I Love With The Gospel Today?

The Great Commission Is Not A Suggestion!

"And He said to them, "Go into all the world and preach the gospel to every creature." (Mk 16:15)

The "World Clock" reports every sixty minutes approximately 7,000 people on the earth die.

According to God's Word, these precious souls will live in one of two places. . . *forever*. Jesus *commanded us* to love people with the Gospel.

In all of our schedules, deadlines, planned meetings, and recreation, it is easy each day to overlook the lost who are everywhere around us.

Yet, they are the reason Jesus came!

"For the Son of Man has come to seek and to save that which was lost." (Lk 19:10)

Every day, ask yourself the question, "Who will I love with the Gospel today?" It doesn't have to be a large number of people, but everyday should count!

A Serious Responsibility

One of the verses in the Bible that continually motivates me for excellence is *". . . For everyone to whom much is given, from him much will be required. . ."* (Lk 12:48b)

When you and I stop to think that we are Christians living in the 21st century, with the greatest means of worldwide communication available, it is staggering!

Never again will sharing the Gospel be limited to just one on one conversation.

Our generation has been given the responsibility and privilege of having hundreds of methods to share God's Word to the masses through modern technology unavailable to any generation of Christians since Jesus!

A Teacher's Surprise

Recently the Holy Spirit brought to my mind a wonderful memory from high school.

In the mid 1980's, the state of Texas conducted annual tests of their high school students.

In 1983, during the administration of this test, many of us were assigned to sit in rooms with teachers who were not our normal instructors.

This particular day, I was sitting in an art class with a teacher I had never met and did not know.

During a break between test sessions, to alleviate boredom, I wrote out John 3:16 on a large piece of paper. "For God so loved the world that He gave His only begotten Son, that whoever believes in Him should not perish but have everlasting life." Moments later, I felt a hand on my shoulder and turned to see the bewildered face of the art teacher. He had obviously read the verse.

His response changed my thinking forever!

With a sincerity and hunger I had never witnessed before, he uttered these words, **"Is that really true?"**

Imagine this precious man, born and raised in Dallas and yet had never heard the wonderful promise of John 3:16! There are millions just like him within hours of your home.

Allow the Holy Spirit to use you today as His messenger on the earth.

Many will never hear the Gospel unless they hear it from you.

Study. . . how to share it.

Master. . . sensitivity to the Holy Spirit.

Expect. . .people to listen and be changed.

Ask the Holy Spirit for a fresh burden for the lost today.

Remember what you make happen for another family, God makes happen for yours!

"Who will I love with the Gospel today?" It is one of the 7 questions you must ask yourself everyday.

Recommended Resource: *7 Lies Christians Believe About the Lost* available in the online bookstore at www.mikesmalley.com

Question 5:
Do I Respect The Laws Of Financial Increase?

Money Is Necessary!

". . . But money answers everything."
(Ecc 10:19b)

Precious few people on the earth have really ever publically communicated the absolute necessity of having financial provision. . . *a lot of money.*

Sadly, many have misunderstood and rejected the financial deliverers sent to the body of Christ.

If you become disrespectful toward money, it will move away from you. Anything you do not respect will begin to exit your life. Anything from a job opening. . . to a new responsibility. . . or a valued and cherished relationship.

People, position, and provision can begin to exit your life when you stop showing respect. . . and they can exit very, very quickly.

You must continually work with your faith and your mind in regards to the law of financial increase.

Money does not go simply where it is needed!

Money goes where it is respected!

What is the proof you respect the financial laws of God?

What is your attitude toward returning the tithe?

What are the last five books you have read on money?

Do you continually keep a list of questions to ask financial mentors?

Are you continually sowing financial seeds into ministries who carry a financial mantle?

A Missed God Opportunity

In 1994, I attended a monthly pastor's luncheon in the Dallas area. The guest speaker that day was Vic Schober, pastor of the great Glad Tidings church in Austin Texas.

I was a young man and on fire for God. I had been meeting monthly, and sometimes weekly, with great men like Leonard Ravenhill for prayer and times of teaching in God's Word.

I arrived at the luncheon hoping for some "meat" from God's Word. I was devastated when Pastor Schober began speaking to us about Mutual Funds!

Pastor Schober was a master in the area of investing and retirement. He pleaded with us to not ignore the warnings of scripture to "lay aside". . . to prepare for winter. . . to save.

I was angered.

I could not believe he "wasted our time" talking to us about money, investing, believing God for financial ideas, and provision.

I Horribly Missed God That Day!

I failed to discern a God moment. . .a Holy Spirit ordained opportunity to respect and embrace a part of God's Word I had not yet discovered.

My disrespect for his Biblical message resulted in my loosing tens of thousands of dollars. Sadly, it was over 10 years before I saw the wisdom of his words.

I lost over a decade to prepare for my future!

You can be a Christian and love God with all of your heart, but struggle financially because of a disrespect for the laws of financial increase.

Never be critical of the voices the Holy Spirit raises up to teach the body of Christ the scriptural ways to prosper. God longs to abundantly bless you. Ask the Holy Spirit to continually plant within you a deep respect for His provision. . . His laws. . . His ideas.

Respect. . . financial mentors.

Study. . .financial laws.

Apply. . .the principles wrapped in your faith.

Expect. . .God to bless you and the work of your hands.

"Do I respect the laws of financial increase?" It is one of the 7 questions you should ask yourself everyday.

Question 6:
Am I Building My Life Around A Pursuit of Wisdom?

Ignorance Is Deadly!

I love knowledge.

As I child, I was unable to even eat a bowl of cereal without voraciously reading every word on the box.

My mind continually aches for Wisdom.

Apparently. . . I am not alone.

For over 30 years, as I have read and studied the biographies of great men of women, one common fact emerges. *They passionately pursued wisdom!*

The Holy Spirit speaking over 3,000 years ago through King Solomon said it best:

"Happy is the man who finds wisdom, And the man who gains understanding. . ." (Prov 3:13a)

Many believe faith is their greatest need. The Bible says otherwise.

"Wisdom is the principal thing; therefore, get wisdom. And in all your getting, get understanding." (Prov 4:7)

Without wisdom, how would I know how to use my faith. . .to grow it. . .to sustain it?

Hosea, the Old Testament prophet, reveals the reason for failure in the lives of God's people.

"My people are destroyed for lack of knowledge."
(Hosea 4:6a)

Sculpture everyday around the pursuit of wisdom. Reach continually. Hourly.

Invest financially in whatever it takes to grow your mind through books, CD's and mentors.

Your Mind Is The Single Most Important Thing In Your Life.

It's more important than your family. It's more important than your spouse. It's more important than your children, because *if you lose your mind, you are going to lose everything else too.*

7 Biblical Rewards Of Wisdom

1. **Profit**
   "For the merchandise of it is better than the merchandise of silver, and the gain thereof than fine gold." (Proverbs 3:14)

2. **Long Life**
   "Length of days is in her right hand. . .
   (Prov 3:16a)

3. **Riches And Honor**
   ". . .In her left hand riches and honor."
   (Prov 3:16b)

4. **Peace**
   ". . . and all her paths are peace."
   (Prov 3:17b)

5. **Happiness**
   "And happy are all who retain her."
   (Prov 3:18b)

6. **Protection**
   "For wisdom is a defense. . ."   (Ecc 7:12a)

7. **Stability** "Wisdom and knowledge will be the stability of your times. . ."   (Is 33:6a)

Build. . . *every day around Wisdom.*

Listen. . . *daily to teaching CD's.*

Read. . . *continually the discovery of others.*

Reach. . . *for the mentorship of champions.*

Master. . . *the art of asking question.*

Write. . . *and journal your discoveries.*

Wisdom's rewards are never ending.

"Am I building my life around the pursuit of wisdom?" It is one of the 7 questions you should ask yourself everyday.

Question 7:
Am I Ready Should I Die Today?

Being Right With God Does Not Make You Ready To Die!

A wise man once said, "Everyone will be a part of the ultimate statistic. . . 10 out of 10 people die."

Every city in every nation contains a cemetery. I have never met anyone who lived in 1541, 1776 or 1812. They are all gone. From the rich to the poor, to the powerful and the weak. . . people die.

Time is a Gift

Every single day, God packages a gift called time and deposits more of it into our life account. Some have decades. . . others seconds.

What we choose to do with the time we are given is a great revealer about who we are.

Pretending we won't die or even believing we could not die today is naïve and ignorant.

The Bible teaches us to expect and believe for a long life, but to prepare for an unexpected exit.

Though the thought of a premature death is an unpleasant thought, it is an issue each of us must face.

I Remember It Like Yesterday

When I was in college, the university required all seniors to do an internship in cooperation with a local church. Mark was the custodian at the church I was privileged to work with. His smile and attitude toward life were contagious. He brought joy and passion to every room he entered.

During my six month internship, it was my honor to share many conversations with Mark. His passion was Christian music. He freely shared his ideas about worship, putting Jesus first and the need for being both bold and urgent in our witness for Christ to the lost.

One morning, I arrived early to the church to be informed by the senior pastor he needed three of the staff to accompany Mark to a city eight hours away to pick up supplies for the church's annual missions convention. I was excited I was asked to go along with Mark. I looked forward to the opportunity to spend eight hours with Mark and the other men of God. The trip was everything I had expected and more! Mark's passion for life and Jesus created a lifetime memory for all of us.

Tragically, several months later, I received the shocking news. Mark had arrived at work complaining of a headache. *Hours later, he collapsed and died.* A brain aneurism had instantly taken this man of God to Heaven.

Mark's death was not only painful since he was such a precious friend, but also because he was in his early 40's. His sudden and tragic death taught me a lifetime lesson. . . *all of us must be prepared to leave!*

Many confuse being ready to meet God with being ready to die. As a minister, it has been my sad duty to conduct the funerals of those who died unexpectedly and then watch their families suffer from their lack of preparation.

Paul told Timothy, *"But if anyone does not provide for his own, and especially for those of his household, he has denied the faith and is worse than an unbeliever."* (1 Tim 5:8)

I believe this verse teaches us to provide for our families even when we are dead!

Good stewardship of our lives not only includes spending our money wisely, it also includes proper preparation for the inevitable. Every Christian needs life insurance and a will.

Through the years, ungodly judges in our court systems have been forced to make decisions concerning estates, guardianship of children and financial distribution because Christians died without their legal house in order. Don't allow the "negative" thoughts about death to keep you from preparing for it properly.

Billy Graham

Billy Graham was once asked if he was afraid to die. I think his reply was brilliant. He said, "I am not afraid to die, but I do fear the dying process."

I think this is true of all who know the Lord. We are not afraid of what happens to us after we die, but none of us look forward to the process of dying.

The Value of a Soul

The reason preparation to die becomes so important is the day we die is the moment we actually begin to live. . .in one of two places.

Jesus, in communicating to us the value of our soul, said it this way, "For what profit is it to a man if he gains the whole world, and loses his own soul? Or what will a man give in exchange for his soul?" (Mt 16:26)

Jesus tells the story of a successful business man who said, "I'll sit back and say to myself, "My friend, you have enough stored away for years to come. Now take it easy! Eat, drink, and be merry!"" "But God said to him, 'You fool! You will die this very night. Then who will get everything you worked for?' (Luke 12:19-20 NLT)

God leaves the preparation for our exit from this life to us. Wisdom never puts off until tomorrow what must be decided today.

Embracing the Cross

The cross continues to be the loudest statement God ever made!

"For God so loved the world that He gave His only begotten Son, that whoever believes in Him should not perish but have everlasting life. For God did not send His Son into the world to condemn the world, but that the world through Him might be saved." (John 3:16-17)

God has made possible for us to have eternal life by placing our trust and faith in what Christ did for us at the cross.

Where we spend eternity will be a result of our own decisions. As we use wisdom and diligence in preparing for a productive life on the earth, let us also return daily to the cross for a fresh encounter with the One who loves us so much He died in our place!

"Am I ready should I die today?" It is one of the 7 questions you should ask yourself everyday.

Have You Invited Christ Into Your Life?

The Bible says, "For all have sinned and fall short of the glory of God." (Rom 3:23)

Sin is breaking God's law - breaking His commandments.

Have you ever lied, lusted, disobeyed your parents or taken something that did not belong to you?

Man's standard is very different from God's. Consider the following verse from Scripture:

"For whoever keeps the whole law and yet stumbles at just one point is guilty of breaking all of it." (James 2:10 NIV)

God's requirement for entry into heaven is perfection. In other words, God's law is like a giant piece of glass. If I drew a circle on the glass and attempted with a hammer to only break that which was inside the circle, all of the glass would shatter!

The heart of our problem is we all have a problem with our heart. Since each of us, by an act of our will have violated our conscience and willingly did what we knew was wrong, we qualify as "sinners" with an imperfect record.

No matter how hard we try, we cannot erase our past sins against God.

The good news is Jesus promised, ". . .the one who comes to Me, I will by no means cast out." (John 6:37b)

Will you turn from sin and ask Jesus Christ into your life right now?

When we turn from a lifestyle of intentional disobedience to God and put our trust in what Christ did at the cross, God gives us the gift of everlasting life.

Pray this prayer:

"Jesus, I've known right from wrong all my life. I have chosen wrong. I have sinned. I need a savior.

I repent and turn from a life of disobeying you. I invite you to come into my life and forgive me of all my sins. I confess with my mouth that Jesus Christ is my Lord and Savior. Fill me with your Spirit. I will read your Word daily and obey what I read.

In Jesus' Name, Amen."

If you have prayed this prayer and desire to learn more about following Jesus, please contact me so I can send you information that will show you what to do next and how to grow as a believer.

Attention: Mike Smalley
Worldreach Ministries
P.O. Box 99
Rockwall, TX 75087
mike@mikesmalley.com
www.mikesmalley.com

About Mike Smalley

- Preached his first public sermon at the age of 14.
- Graduated from Southwestern University in 1992.
- Pastored near Dallas from 1992-1998
- Began full-time evangelism at the age of 30, which has continued since 1998.
- Has started over 45 churches overseas.
- Spoken to more than 4,000 audiences in 25 countries, including Asia, East Africa, the Orient, and Europe.
- Noted author of 9 books, including, *Saved Soul Wasted Life, 10 Master Rewards for Sitting Daily In The Presence Of God, 7 Questions You Must Ask Yourself Everyday and How to Jumpstart Your Prayer Life* and more.
- Hosts the worldwide daily Internet Television broadcast, "Wisdom for Achievers."
- Has appeared on TBN, Daystar, LeSea and numerous other television network programs.
- Has embraced his assignment to *Preach the Gospel to the Lost and Equip Christians In The Wisdom of God.*
  - Is Founder and President Of Worldreach Ministries, based in Rockwall Texas.

Join Worldreach 1000 Today!

My Dear Friend,

I don't believe it was an accident God connected you to this book. I have asked the Holy Spirit for 1000 partners who will plant a monthly Seed of $66 to help me spread the Gospel across the earth. (66 represents the 66 books in the Word of God.)

Will you become my Monthly Partner in the Worldreach 1000?

Your monthly sponsorship Seed of $66 will not only impact millions across the earth, but will also create a personal harvest back to you.

3 harvests you should expect:
1. Divine Health (Psalms 41:1-3)
2. Divine Favor (Luke 6:38)
3. The 100 Fold Return (Mark 10:28-30)

Yours for Wisdom,

Evangelist Mike Smalley

P.S. Log onto www.mikesmalley.com and visit the online store to enroll in the *Worldreach 1000*. Or, you may call 24 hours a day 1-866-96-SOULS. Be sure to request your special partners appreciation gift pack, full of my books and teaching CDs.

One Final Thought

If this book has changed your life, I'd love to hear from you!

Additional copies of this book may be ordered for a friend, small group, or co-workers on your job.

Remember nothing changes people like the Wisdom of God!

Quantity Discount Price List:

7 Questions You Should Ask Yourself Everyday

(B-09)

Quantity	Cost Each	Discount
1- 9	$10 each	None
10-49	$7 each	30%
50-249	$6 each	40%
250-999	$5 each	50%
1000 & up	$4 each	60%

WISDOM FOR ACHIEVERS TELEVISION

Watch Mike teach LIVE every

Monday – Thursday

on Internet Television!

To view a *broadcast schedule*,
join the *LIVE teachings*,
or watch *archived broadcasts*,
visit our website at:

www.mikesmalley.com

SPECIAL OFFER!

As special way of saying "Thank You" for investing in a copy of *7 Questions You Should Ask Yourself Everyday,* I'd like to offer you a few FREE gifts.

- FREE one year subscription to Mike Smalley's Inner Circle e-Mentorship program. You will receive 2 teaching emails each week mentoring you in your walk with God.
- An audio of Dr. Smalley's dynamic teaching, *How To Turn Tragedies Into Triumphs.*
- One of Dr. Smalley's most popular eBooks. Truly life changing!

Ready to receive your FREE gifts?

**Simply email now your name and preferred email address to
<u>specialoffer@mikesmalley.com</u>
and ask for your "7 Questions" special offer!
You may also call 972-771-3339.**